Bibliographic information published by the German National Library:

The German National Library lists this publication in the National Bibliography; detailed bibliographic data are available on the Internet at http://dnb.dnb.de .

Imprint:

Copyright © 2017 GRIN Verlag, Open Publishing GmbH
Print and binding: Books on Demand GmbH, Norderstedt Germany
ISBN: 9783668527416

This book at GRIN:

http://www.grin.com/en/e-book/373667/data-mining-algorithms-its-functions-and-structure

Junaid Khan, Wajeeh Ahmed

Data Mining Algorithms, its Functions and Structure

A comparitive study

GRIN Publishing

GRIN - Your knowledge has value

Since its foundation in 1998, GRIN has specialized in publishing academic texts by students, college teachers and other academics as e-book and printed book. The website www.grin.com is an ideal platform for presenting term papers, final papers, scientific essays, dissertations and specialist books.

Visit us on the internet:

http://www.grin.com/

http://www.facebook.com/grincom

http://www.twitter.com/grin_com

DATA MINING AND ITS APPLICATIONS: A COMPARATIVE STUDY

BY JUNAID ZIA KHAN

WAJEEH AHMED

Abstract

We live in a world which contains an enormous amount of data that grows every day and is at our disposal. Whether it comes from social media, the internet, or file records. We wouldn't be very bright, if we didn't find ways to manipulate and use this data so that we could extract patterns and information from it. One of the ways to extract patterns and use data in an intelligent way is through the use of data mining.

Data mining has evolved throughout the years and has grown to become an immensely powerful tool. Researchers use it for the same purposes. There are two classes of data mining algorithms, from the arsenal of algorithms, you can majorly use classification algorithms or clustering procedures. When work is done through data mining, the accuracies of the results are also published at times. We are dedicated in this research paper to analyze the accuracies that researchers publish and hopefully get better results by conducting similar tests on samples that we find from a well-known repository of machine learning datasets and try and hypothesize why one algorithm performs better than another.

In other papers, we have simply given our recommendations after reading the processes that the researchers have taken, in order for them to improve their work and hopefully implement some of our suggestions into what it is they are doing.

Analysis

We were tasked with the problem of checking the accuracies and the performance of some of the algorithms that were used in the predictive analysis sense. And we decided that there was no better platform to test our theory than on the free, open-source platform, Knime. We had to create simple workflows that got data from a well-known repository for machine learning, and we used the data sets uploaded there to aid in our research. We wanted to check how performance varied across data-mining algorithms. Then using a CSV file reader and an all-important partitioning node, we set the training and testing split to be at 70/30 percent, that is, the data used in the file would account as, 70 percent would go to train the nodes present in our workflow and the other 30 percent would go to the predictive node. We also enabled random seeding, so that the records that were being taken were done so in a random manner ensuring better accuracy and a higher probability of getting accurate results. Then we went off the list of both classification and clustering algorithms, such as decision trees, random forest, gradient boosted trees, k nearest neighbors, support vector machines, naïve Bayes and the likes and after training the data, and waiting patiently for the nodes to be fully configured, some requiring more time than others, which is due to the functioning and the mechanism of each algorithm which we will explain later on in the paper, we executed the nodes after getting the green signal, and attached a method of visually representing our results. So, we attached a scorer at the end of each algorithms workflow, which would score our results and return two things, a confusion matrix and an accuracy table.

We weeded out the errors and the null pointer exceptions in most cases and found that the results which we were getting were faring off better than the ones in the research paper. This might be due to the fact that we had a data set of varying size in both cases or because of the functioning of each algorithm. We recorded the results that we got in tables which we have presented here.

We found in cancer research that the paper that we read, we did the same research using a different data set, and found that we received an accuracy of 97.6 through support vector machines.

We also did cross-checking of the values indicated in the human resources research paper and found that we got a value of 98.6 through random forest which was astonishingly high, while the lowest score of any algorithm tested was 83.2 through naïve bayes.

The values and accuracies that we got compared to the cancer research:

Random forest- Training testing split, 70/30	97.6
k-nearest neighbor –	97.1
decision tree-	94.3
svm-	97.6
naïve bayes-	95.2
gradient boosted learner-	94.3

The accuracies that we got compared to the human resources research:

Method	Accuracy
naïve bayes=	83.2
decision trees –	97.6
gradient boosted tree-	97.6
random forest -	98.6
tree ensemble -	98.5
k-nearest -	94.6

For the first two research papers we conducted extensive research in order to compare our results with theirs and we used knime and the uci repository to garner our own information where we could make educated guesses about why an algorithm worked and why it fared off better than other algorithms. We found that our results were much better as compared to the ones found in the research paper. We reflected on why some algorithms were acting the way they were and why there was discrepancy in between the algorithms used. We know that there are some algorithms that take an excessive amount of time to train and some work differently than

Breast Cancer Prediction: (MERARYSLAN MERALIYEV 2. Z., 2017)

The dataset used for demonstration was comprised of 699 entries and the features used were Clump Thickness, Uniformity of cell size, Uniformity of cell shape, Marginal Adhesion, Single Epithelial cell size, Bare Nuclei, Bland Chromatin, Normal Nucleoli, Mitoses. Since there are not a lot of features involved, feature selection was not necessary. The algorithms tested in the research were the C4.5 variant of the decision tree, K-nearest neighbors, Naive Bayes and Support Vector Machines with accuracy scores of 94.3, 97.1, 95.2, 97.6 respectively. The overall best performer was the SVM algorithm and our tests do indeed confirm that is the case. The data was partitioned using a randomly sampled 70/30 split for training/testing. We tested 2 additional algorithms, Random Forest classifier and Gradient Boosted Tree classifier and they returned accuracy scores of 97.6 and 94.3 respectively. The Random Forest classifier gives comparable accuracy to the SVM and requires less time to train however is slower than an SVM at prediction although the parity is marginal. The dataset in it's entirety is composed of numerical values and the Support Vector Machine is a non-probabilistic classifier that operates best on numerical values and hence the excellent accuracy scores were therefore expected. The other algorithms all operate on categorical values and as a result the accuracy while still not as bad does suffer. Since the problem comprises of data that is continuous in nature, it is generally not wise to consider a classifier that relies on categorical features. The Support Vector Machine operates by building a decision boundary separating the data by it's class and mapped onto a higher-dimensional space where the dimensions are essentially the features of the data that are to be taken into consideration when making the classification. Decision Trees and it's variants while providing respectable accuracy should not be chosen in such situations because of their nature of operation on continuous inputs. Accuracy in cancer prediction is a very serious concern and whatever classifier is chosen, features and applicability should be accounted for in the given context. Naive Bayes classifier uses a probability function to estimate the output prediction and by nature operates on categorical inputs. Continuous values are treated as categorical inputs and this not only increases the time needed to make a classification but because the probability and sample distribution generated from training the classifier cannot operate properly on continuous inputs I.e values that may not be available in the probability distribution, the Naive Bayes classifier is prone to significant errors. Our recommendation is the use of the Support Vector Machine classifier or a joint ensemble classification system where classifiers are stacked together similar to Random Forests. The test we ran confirmed our findings that indeed the support vector machine that although takes longer to train is the best predictor with a very low rate of error and high prediction speeds.

Churn prediction

Employee churn and retention is often a major concern for corporations and repeated surveys on employee satisfaction often get annoying and when employees suddenly leave especially valuable ones, it is often a setback for the company so machine learning can be a better indicator of employee satisfaction than the general manager and thats what is highlighted by research papers published on this matter. The dataset we used was composed of Last Evaluation date, Number of Projects worked on, Average monthly hours, Time spent at the company, Whether they had a work accident, Whether they had a promotion in the last 5 years, Department, Salary. And this information is used to predict if the company will retain the employee for the next term of will the employee leave before the next term. This is Employee Retention or Churn Analysis. We evaluated Naive Bayes, C4.5 Decision Trees, Gradient Boosted Trees, Random Forest, Tree Ensemble and K-Nearest-Neighbours that gave us scores of 83.2, 97.6, 97.6, 98.6, 98.5, 94.6 etc. The Random Forest gave the overall best accuracy score because when employees leave or stay the factors involved usually have a correlated pattern that forms over time and trees are very effective at modelling predictions based on patterns because patterns are effectively what treees are composed off. Probabilistic classifiers are expected to perform well but their probabilistic nature makes them unpredictable so the efficacy of the classifier solely depends on the training data fed into it as well as the nature of the algorithm itself. We recommend ensemble methods for predicting employee churn such as the Ensemble Tree which in our test scores the best overall.

SENTIMENT ANALYSIS (wakade, 2010)

Sentiment Analysis isn't always done for fun but also is a very valuable tool for evaluating the performance of a company and it's products. The term itself is very broad and covers a wide range of areas but the area we have explored and worked on is merely classification of opinions into negative or positive classes. The dataset comprises of movie reviews from the IMDB database and there are 5000 in total. There are various steps involved in processing the data such as removing emoticons and unnecessary symbols, stemming which reduces the words down to their roots, filtering stop-words that are essentially words which do not and finally converting the words to vectors using word2vec which is basically a 2 layer neural network that takes the words as inputs and outputs a vector containing relative scores of occurrence of the words in each document or instance passed into the first layer. Finally all the results were fed into a C4.5 tree that resulted in an accuracy of 62% which although not very impressive but given the nature of that data which is very unpredictable and sparse is still a satisfactory performer. Probabilistic classifiers cannot perform well in this sort of environment because not all words used in an opinion maybe present in the probability distribution of the Naive-bayes model. Our recommendation is to use an ensemble classifier such as Random Forest for such tasks because of the way this classifier deals with incorrect classifications and tuning of the next generated tree in the model.

There were other research papers where the accuracies of the algorithms used were not mentioned nor was mentioned where the dataset used in the research paper came from, so we have recommendations for those papers instead of having conducted extensive analysis, where we compared our results with theirs in terms of accuracies and came up with hypothesizes about why the accuracies obtained were so.

You'll find that if these recommendations implemented into the systems and the applications of these respective papers, they would greatly increase the usability of the applications and remove the need of unnecessary workarounds such as is the case with the papers on shazam and privacy-protecting data mining. Although, these recommendations are just our opinions and we do not know whether the things suggested require extensive and grueling effort or if they are simple to implement into these systems.

PRIVACY PROTECTING DATA MINING (A., 1999)

In the previous research paper about privacy-protecting data mining, we found that they highlighted the need for privacy-protecting data mining and how people are more fearful of divulging information onto the internet because they fear that it might be misused or profiles can be kept on them where their personal details and behavioral patterns aren't safe. And this is true, because data mining can be used for malicious intent, it is a field that is very powerful and can be used to predict and come up with and maintain profiles on particular people which could endanger them and be used to keep tabs on them or for other malicious intent.

The workings of this research paper are so that they used two methods to obscure the data and change the true value of the data, which are the best ways to go about protecting data. They added a random value to the actual data which obscured it and secondly they also created a range in which the user inputted the data instead of putting in real values in order to protect the information. Another thing the researchers could have done was if they encrypted the data in order for it to be useless to those people who wanted to use it for malicious intent. They could use encryption as a means to protect the data as it is one of the principles of cybersecurity and that would have eliminated the need to go through extensive obscuring of data through data discretization.

They further used decision trees to train the data and predict it, therefore when the data to be trained was sent in the form of having been obscured, the results that came out of it were unable to be used to trace back to original values.

We believe that this was the best approach to go about protecting ones data and ensuring safety on the internet.

SHAZAM (wang, 2003)

There was another research paper about shazam, this is a technology for those who are not familiar, returns results where it gives you the name and artist of the song that it is being played. And you need to feed it an audio file, either upload it or record it through your phone and send it directly over through a call, and shazam uses its technology which uses music data mining to return the name and artist of the song being played. This is a great app for those of you who don't know the name of the song but have access to the song.

So, how the technology works is that it intakes the audio file and compares it to an existing database where it has already separated the peaks or the highest and lowest points in the music's audio graph. It calculates the distance between these peaks and matches it to the song file uploaded onto its server. There it uses combinatorial hashing and clustering algorithms to find out similarity between the song being played and its existing database and returns the result.

Another use of classification algorithms in music data mining, is the use of classification algorithms in finding out the genre of the music.

We feel that this approach of calculating peaks and then plotting them on a graph in order to implement hashing on them is the best approach in the case of shazam, although there could be additional features that could be added to it to make it more resourceful.

The developers could have a functionality in the software where if the person, if they know the lyrics to the song can text or upload their presumed lyrics or affirmed lyrics and the database could use dynamic programming to find out which song the lyrics belong to or are the most similar to, because at times the user does not have access to the song or they don't remember the tune. The principle of edit distance can be used to find out similarities in the users guess and the existing database of lyrics. Edit distance is an algorithm which is extensively used in finding out how close a phrase or sentence is in relation to another phrase or sentence by calculating a score and doing an exhaustive search, the further use of dynamic programming reduces the recursiveness of the algorithm and it provides a more optimal solution.

The limited role of counterterrorism in data-mining. (Harper, 2006)

This research paper caused a lot of discussion amongst us. As it was very contradictory as it seemed, to the modern use of data mining and its applications in the field of terrorism.

This research paper dictates how data mining cannot be used in the field of counterterrorism, which is a field where people try to find ways to battle terrorism, simply because of some technical faults which are fundamental to the field of data mining.

It highlights how other crimes such as theft, and money laundering occur very frequently throughout the year, and so these crimes are recorded and there is sufficient data on them. Sufficient data means accurate results and valid results when someone plans to use this data for data mining. That is to say, because there is a large repository of information, data mining techniques and algorithms can be applied on them easily and it will return an accurate result.

It also highlights, that in contrast to these crimes, how terrorism and terrorist attacks and activities are such events that only occur sparsely, if ever, throughout the year. And because they are so sparse and far-apart, there is not much one can do to gather a large repository of data on them. And so, if the data that you are working with is small in size, in this case, too small, it cannot be used for data mining, as it will always return incorrect results.

My group member then made an effort to highlight the fact that this is not true, and that data mining is extensively used in predicting the next events to occur.

Twitter and social media can be used to predict the next area under attack by terrorist activities.

Visualization data mining (Keim, 2002)

Visualization data mining is a new field of data mining where a subject has to be immersed into the data process, instead of simply using statistical means to calculate patterns. There are many ways to approach data mining, one way to do that is visually. Visual data mining takes data mining to another level by integrating unique and new graphs into visually representing the data. The study comprises of using basic and traditional methods of representation of data such as bar graphs and scatterplots. But also introduces a whole new array of representing data such as pixels and nested graphs. Everything from hyperlinks, to 2 dimensional data and multidimensional data is analyzed in this field of study. Multidimensional data meaning data with many attributes such as relational databases. 2 dimensional data such as maps and graphs, and one dimensional data such as a single field. These can be represented through various way, 2 d data can be represented through graphs, and 3d data can be represented through topologies.

We would recommend that a way to measure the data when it comes to hyperlinks is word length, and number of conjunctions or dashes. Through harnessing the power of pixels, we can represent data as well. There are a million pixels on our computer screen and if we allocate a single data field to each one we can cluster them and find out points of concentration by analyzing the different colors that they show.

Web usage mining (J., 2002)

Instead of finding out patterns in the data and figuring out and predicting the next big thing, web usage mining is the field of study where data mining techniques are applied to maintain profiles or identities about the users or customers of a website, product or business. What kinds of interests they have and what behaviors they exhibit are all things that are covered in web usage mining.

Things from hypertext markup language, to text and images are analyzed and turned into useful information to gather intelligence on the customers of a service.

Through this type of data mining, you can actually give your customers personalized web pages, since you have maintained profiles on them and you know their likes and their dislikes and their interests.

We would suggest that to further this research, social computing should be integrated in this type of mining with the use of sentiment analysis and the resulting data should be used in recommender systems, since they are also systems that recommend users what to buy and suggest things to them. An example of a recommender system would be YouTube, where a suggested videos link pops up on the side of the screen with results collected for you based on your previous video browsing.

Big data mining (Wu, 2010)

In the modern world, there is an influx of large amounts of data that can be utilized to predict patterns and behaviors. But in order to do that, we need the proper hardware to process this information. Data warehouses are too small to hold and capture the datasets that are native to big data. So NoSQL databases such as Hadoop are used to harbor all the information. This is actually a problem with databases, if they are not scalable, they result in failure, i.e., if they cannot grow and accommodate more users then they won't be useful, because there is a constant need for accommodating more fields and data inside a database. Anyhow, this data is then utilized, in machine learning, predictive analytics and data mining, and is used to predict future events, patterns that were not being seen before etc.

Bioinformatics (Frank)

Data mining can be applied to the field of medical sciences as well. With the increase in more complex predictive queries and tasks, manual labor fails to keep at par with the increasing need to predict and analyze a great amount of data. Therefore, we need computers to aid us in this matter, and one of the ways to do that is through data mining. Data mining, can be used to predict the structure of genes and proteins by reading the genomic sequence of nucleotides. It can also be used to predict the function of genes as well. Our suggestion is to use data mining in the study of the human genome, as that is one project that if implemented in, could not only help in identifying what most genes are doing but it could probably help us in making a breakthrough in the field of medical sciences.

Text mining (wakade, 2010)

Text mining, includes the study of text and the implementation of data mining techniques on it. Sentiment analysis is implemented through mining text. Text is one of the most fundamental sources of information on the internet and occurs in abundance. Therefore finding ways to harness this data is an important task.

CONCLUSION

In the cancer prediction case we found out that the data is almost always going to be comprised of continuous values so using a probabilistic classifier such as naive-Bayes or pattern based classifier such as a tree may not always yield the best performance. A non-probabilistic, unbiased classifier such as the SVM is the most optimally performing classifier in our tests is our recommendation for classification of data derived of continuous features.

In sentiment analysis, the data is usually very sparse, unstructured and may contain a lot of noise that may confuse the classifier, additionally probabilistic classifiers are biased towards the majority entry in the feature space and hence cannot deal effectively with inputs not available in the trained probability distribution. Our recommendation is to use either a neural network but that will almost always be extremely slow in training. Another suitable classifier is the Random Forest because opinions whether positive or negative follow a pattern in words so certain words can be given increased weight than the rest and when fed into an ensemble classifier such as this one, the performance can be very satisfactory.

In Churn Prediction whether employees retain or leave, the factors involved usually have an identifiable pattern and a pattern following classifier such as a decision tree or one of its variants can be an excellent performer in such a scenario. Our recommendation is the Random Forest because of its efficacy in tuning the trees generated and boosting the misclassified records to tune the trees.

11

References

big data analytics. (n.d.). Retrieved from http://searchbusinessanalytics.techtarget.com: http://searchbusinessanalytics.techtarget.com/definition/big-data-analytics

Jeff Jonas and Jim Harper, *effective counterterrorism and the limited role of data mining.* (2006).

Frank, E. (2004). *Data mining in bioinformatics using Weka.*

Harper, J. J. (2006). *Effective Counterterrorism and the limited role of data mining.*

Keim, D. A. (2002.). *Information Visualization and Visual Data Mining.*

MERARYSLAN MERALIYEV, 2. Z. (2017). CHOOSING BEST MACHINE LEARNING ALGORITHM FOR BREAST CANCER.

Rakesh Agrawal, (1999) *privacy preserving data mining.*

Shruti Wakade, (2010), Text Mining for Sentiment Analysis of Twitter Data.

shazam entertainment. (2003). Wang.

Srivastava, J. (2000). *Web Usage Mining: Discovery and Applications of Usage.*

text mining. (n.d.). Retrieved from wikipedia: https://en.wikipedia.org/wiki/Text_mining

WAJDI, D. (2000.). *DATA MINING IN bioinformatics.*

Web mining. (n.d.). Retrieved from Wikipedia, : https://en.wikipedia.org/wiki/Web_mining

WEB USAGE MINING. (n.d.). Retrieved from http://www.web-datamining.net/usage/

Wu, X. (2010.). *Data Mining with Big Data.*